FOURTH FLOW PRESS
An imprint of Fluid Hive LLC
Fluid Hive LLC, PO Box 2314
Alexandria, VA 22301 USA

Copyright © Dawan Stanford, 2010
All Rights Reserved

Library of Congress Control Number: 2014948920
ISBN 9780984886906

# FEVER MUSIC

**◐**₁

**one**₅

**two**₁₉

**four**₅₃

**three**₃₃

**five**₆₃

**six**₈₅

**●**₁₀₉

*white, green, brown*

When I feel your bones are hollow
it does not mean you are
my little bird or that you
have not perched on my body
or that I have not been the happy flea
warm in your feathers and your flight.
If I feel your bones are hollow
against mine they are all hollow trees
that still sprout green in springtime.
You unfurl and pour your body.
I hear hollows calling.  The bees in me,
the squirrels, all the nesting things,
turn their heads.

# one

*Flutter*

Her mouth
          should have been
  a machine:
      a wood chipper or nuclear plant,
something dangerously efficient.
    Her mouth
  shouldn't have been
         designed
  to place expert
     and indifferent kisses:
flames refusing to burn
     a Promethean moth.

*coming over*

I have a spider in my ear.
She has red eyes and blue teeth
because that is how I want
to see her.  Her legs rattle
and scrape when I turn my head.
Her belly thumps against me
when she tires of waiting.
It is only your promise of vice
that makes her still and stealthy,
crouched against my brain
where her hunter's poise
leaks into my thoughts.

*My Amoral Sweet*

An obscene smear
follows and anticipates
your presence.
I can smell ripe fruit
in your wake and
close proximity
woos small hairs
on my arms and neck
with static electric cooing.
You move on feet
and hooves and claws
and fins and feathers.
You coax the cave
from my mind's
limbic swamp and
take me back to nights
before our brain
corrupted flesh
with an abundance of light.

*framed and hung: until*

having survived your killing jar
and the pins spreading and presenting,
a small head and smaller pecker
bang against glass

that killing jar is a
        techno-ethno-socio
                logical marvel
it smells and tastes like things
you will always miss about home
it touches you like your lover
its whispers cause only smiles
it is absolutely modern

framed
*(tap tap tap)*
and you hear
*tap tap tap*
occasionally, like a mosquito
hunting above your heart
and you don't know
where to swat

*Bidden Mistral*

Skin cells signal impatience
like miles of children
queuing for a single smile
worn then passed to the next.
Her whisper mutes a
crowded room, echoes
in her and marches
out brisk and baritone.
Her serenade, needle rain,
labels her pain.  The schematic
reads touch here, then here,
then maps wiring around
burnt resistors and blown capacitors.
Her diagram hides her
function, but solenoids,
diodes, motors, and gears
coruscate and draw
the wry tinkerer near.

*the breath before*

His small and efficient vehicle,
brought to a halt, gives them
to each other
through the passenger window.
He keeps both liver-spotted hands
on the wheel while she grips
the door, palms two fists apart.
His nails are clean and unseen.
Her nails have light pink polish
splashing over onto the cuticles.
Leaning in, her hair hides a face
made up just for him.  He is bald
and obstructing traffic.  Her bare stomach
is flat and his hangs over his belt.
The light is still green.  A small wave
hangs above smooth rocks.  A moth
floats motionless near a street lamp.
Their mouths are open to speak,
taking in the breath before
they share a first sound.
Nothing has been bought or sold
though the transaction is complete.

# two

*Natural History*

CAREFREE   HELD   CRADLED
—all the good stuff
on high shelves
in vats and jars.
Hands roam taps
touching, turning, traipsing
like rodents' paws
on warm pillows.
These soft fingers
stalk the shelves,
caressing yes
from metal limbs;
it rushes out below
from pert and puckered
lips open as to suckle
in the terminal "O" of no.
These bodies may not survive.
Bones, and the skin that serves,
mingle like breath in breath.
This is so easy, so light.

*Postscript to the History of Fire*

that you were mud
I might
could easily
wait in you
sink in
and wait until
sun cracked you
down to my cocoon
and let me visit
my abandoned world
on what light invades
the fissures in yours
that you were mud
I might, I would

but you are stone
and stone on stone
makes sparks, makes heat
makes of our caresses

dust

particulate affection

that our night voices
carry away commingled

*Vieux Nice & Lover*

She signed seeds
memory calls longing
with night-alley footsteps
shifted imperceptibly predatory
by muting autumn mist.
Yellow street lights
shed thread for her
to stitch the room
into a patchwork paradise
as fragile as spider architecture
and similar in function.
Happy prey he was then.
Happy prey. Ancient brick walls
and exposed ceiling beams
succumbed to her gravity
and surrendered
one hundred years
witnessing ways a woman
leaves a man hovering
near constant want.

*Pilgrimage*

Shrouded fingers run
the marathons of Lilliput
where sand from a broken
hourglass collects in hills
on her skin.  There they
remember when falling
was accounting for time.  There's
nothing here that wasn't carried
on backs or smuggled in blood.
This geography gives footprints
a restful interval
before selling them out
to moan tectonics.  Even spies
on this journey bear
irreproachable faith in touch.

*proximate cause*

Welcome to the neighborhood.
        you should come—
                family drinks food
        would be nice to meet—
                holidays visiting visiting
Did you meet
        their daughter?
        their son?

You're meeting for drinks.  How nice.
You're having dinner.  How . . . nice.

Two adult children later heard
at separate times, most likely
in similar suburban kitchens,
"Be nice, (he's/she's)
the neighbor's (son/daughter),"
as if a body briefly sheltering
a body were some kind of theft;
as if you can call someone
stuffing sweets into their pants
while the cashier lends a hand
a shoplifter.  Whatever title fits,
say it with a smile
for the adult children
who had a nice time playing.

*0.0.0*

The *x-axis*
ran its imaginary line
through her womb
until markings and numbers
disappeared into her hips—
positive on the right,
negative on the left.
The *y-axis* anchored
in her head and
traversed her clitoris
or anus depending
on how she arranged
her spine. The *z-axis*
could place you
in front or behind her
but never properly inside.
Each axis told lies that
let her be solid and
reducible to polygons,
numbers, and vectors.
Each axis let her
be liquid consenting
to holding one form
and being held.
The cracked riverbed
in my skin
echoes her curves and force,
raises tiny smiles
under my fingers
when I trace
what was prophesied
by the trickle,
splash, and gush
her first kiss
played in my mouth.

# three

*yesterday's apprentice*

Yesterday's apprentice
knows
his mate
when she makes
arms of his wings,
skin of his scale,
eyes of his antenna,
bones of his metal frame.
She knows him
when he unfolds
and refolds her flesh
carefully, as with
her own hands.
Their touch transmutes,
makes each
for the other,
returns each
to something
a pulse can
recognize and desire.
The growl and hiss
falls from their voices
but years
of forbidden alchemy
make them speak
rushing-water vowels
and crushed-leaf consonants.
Their scarred voices
are never shy
though sometimes
silence serves them better.

*sous-chef*

He eats too much. A man,
yes, it must be male.
Gluttony trembles in his jowls.
He gorges, binges, celebrates
his excess appetite. His face
sweats and glistens, is always slick.
Greed lashes him filthy.
A dirty thing this man.
A pig this man, slurping and snorting
his hog sonata. This man,
together with his hunger
a beast consuming hunger,
always in salt sweet savor.
Late-winter wolves
feast with great repose compared
to this thing whose muffled snarls
confess to being
stitched of craving and want
by the thighs on his cheeks,
the hips in his hands,
and her glistening mouth
answering him silently from its folds
   *feed  feed  feed*

*Irrefragable*

Nails descending,
she made a song
for drunken crickets
on taut denim over
his interred intention.
One button.
Metal teeth unknitted.
Her hooked finger
pulled out and away.
It sprang up
into morning's
blue-gray womb
like a switchblade
filling a hollow
night alley
with a wicked
finger of light.

*Venture*

Witnessing
your tight climax,
knotted back muscles and
near sub-sensory hip twitch,
knocked me out of orbit.
My satellite spun away
firing pathetic thrusts
against new momentum
destined for foreign gravity's
indifferent claws.
I drifted and relayed data,
whispering patiently
into blackness
though intervals
between your replies
grew steadily longer
and your voice
increasingly thin.

*between bodies*

My fingers smell
of garlic, onion and semen.
It was a good dinner.
I'm looking forward
to finishing the half-bottle
of red after you leave
and to waking up alone.
You'll be on my sheets,
pillow and skin
dragging me by the nose
toward my body
that vanishes when you leave.
For now, I have that body
with our sweat in its navel.
You bite my shoulder and
I yelp, as happy now
as I will be tomorrow
in my other flesh.

*Obsidian Fingernails*

Obsidian fingernails show a body
its ballast.  Putsch and pogrom slip
into caresses offered up
by obsidian-tipped fingers—
they know a body's apple core
cradles seeds between
a flowering's cicatrix
and a stem's failure.  Seeds
remember how to rebuild a body,
how to hang a broken jaw
or lay down a map of moles.
A lover's hand on seed-flesh
enters its potent dreaming, splices desires
and confessions to the coded nectar
charting the body's awakening
in the fertile interval
after the embrace.

*Sarah Said*

*there are moments when I love you*

You coax me, always almost
con me, into bed
where I am a meal
the chefs labored over
for years.
Your mouth learned flavor
taking me in.  Your body
made itself the flower
consuming a myth
about a seed-shaped me.
Stomach, intestines—you
pecked at me, pulled from me,
sifted and selected.  Now, reduced
I'm in your rectum
pounding your anus
for a little light to release me
from all you kept.

*of small machines*

sandpaper kiss
acetylene tongue
and you keep returning
to show me
wires and gears
nested penumbral and
glittering golden
on your retractable soul

our intersecting affections
form a blistered lacunae
and you keep coming back,
falling with me,
purchasing symbiosis
with our effacing abyss,
giving me, briefly,
the gift of quickening
two bodies
flung out of orbit,
a weary two-skin satellite
conscripted,
mission unnamed

*Two Myths*

A rare blue crab periodically
chips away its entire shell.
For several days, it moves as squids move
and is defenseless against predators,
rough surfaces, and even its own kind.
Sudden water temperature shifts
shock its exposed nervous system.
Direct sunlight kills.  Outside the water,
the crab's cream, orange, and blue-gray flesh
tears itself apart for want of buoyancy.
Immersed in fatal biology, those males and females
without shells separating self from world
are briefly able to seek and find.
They entwine legs and bodies
into a single violent ball.  Dull amber eggs
float fertilized from the pulsating mass.
Bundled in mating, each crab secretes
what its partner needs to knit a new shell.

These crabs don't exist.  And who are we
to say they don't exist when we extrude bones
during each nocturnal cycle
where tongue rolls and flickers over tongue.

# four

*He Calls Apocalypse*

Watching his lover sleep,
he was, every few seconds,
creation's fiercest enemy
and a smiling assassin
at his soul's throat.
He was repeatedly pinned out alive,
like the last Monarch butterfly
struggling against
an eager lepidopterist.
She could not see him
snared in the cruel interval
where her exhalation ended
and inhalation had yet
to absolve his ardor
for inciting momentary apostasy.
She could not hear him
speak this dialect of love.

*leaving*

The last time we made love
I briefly felt tears
rattle in your body and kept moving.
I covered each surfacing shudder
with my weight and heat
and forced each salty head
down beneath your waters,
down toward a gentle smothering—
moneys for a mind in exile,
a world's better world.
I carry your belly's
sudden quake in mine;
its bitter tincture is as sweet
as all the lust it exceeds.

*her knees*

There's nothing more profound here
      than the woman
on her knees
      sucking and gagging and feeling
oak and maple parquet
      bite her skin.
He hopes
      she is uncomfortable
            —a little pain
      for a thirsty stone altar.
He weaves his hands
      into her hair,
cradling her skull
      and cuddling into
her throat.
He leans in
      and she struggles
           for and against
the act.
      When his mind's image lab
washes away
      his irreal world
with skin,
      he leans into
           two fistfuls of hair
so she will not see
      him evaporate,
see his taking taking taking.

*driving to work after a one-night stand*

Hard candy's melting edges
carved its initials in a mouth's
soft and yielding surfaces
before teeth could rush
the stinging consummation
to its end.  Blood and sugar
are the only evidence
of seeking, finding, devouring.
Blood and sugar are the only voice
a small body's crystalline lattice
gave to reticence and willingness.
An evening dissolving.  A sheet
stretched flat.  A wet footprint
evaporating.  Sound brought down
like lame deer.  Blood and sugar
keep everything fresh and sharp
even after we swallow.

# five

*climbing*

love the fallen,
those who gambled and lost
and still smile
all broken teeth and rubble

love them gently and listen
for voices you recognize
written in scars
and silence where you see
a silver arc glistening
on a stunned tongue

they are like fallen leaves—
spring's good evidence;
take them on your backs
or in your arms

they know stone faces
where flatness and the below
make crevices and ridges
lie to numbing fingers and toes

they'll cover your ears
with what they were
and hoped to be
when icy winds sing
to wings you haven't won:
*it's so easy*
       *easier than letting go*
*lighter than*
       *the lightest thing you've carried*

*Decaying Orbit*

Nestled in bed,
she reinvents skin,
oscillating divine, even
from the cheap seats.
So I steal down past ushers and
bodyguards and pick the lock
on the gold-starred door.
I walk past her clothes
and her *no* and descend
like fog, sealing her resistance
inside her slumber. I violate her
dreams, making myself a groom,
father, friend, or aging hand
in hers. I take my time and
see her without crenellated battlements,
see her open and whole. I store small
pieces of her as patches. She always leaves
my sheets with tremulous haste, cutting speed.
The comfort she takes in closing my door
leaves a hissing hole in my satellite.

*Long Exposure*

Inside a human silhouette
you have everything—cities, stars,
tides, asphalt, leaves—except light.
The world's edges fall over
into this dark body.  This body
sheds a dimension.  This thin flesh,
offers a shadow-filled well
that can show you anything
if it embraces light the right way.
You laughed at my little camera
while posing naked by the window.
Running late for your flight,
you helped me keep our words
in their scabbards and holsters
by posing.  "Your flash is broken.
They'll never come out."
The shutter opened. "Yes, I know."
And closed.

*Fidelity*

Rolling over to hold you
in my half-sleep
just before dawn,
I spilled red wine
over the room service menu
and down over the Gideons'
little bomb in the open drawer.
She started, stirred,
and curled in behind me,
placed her nose on my spine.
Every bed opens a chasm.
My forgetful body
bridges worlds so I take
a bed's left side with her
and its right side with you.

*how to catch a falling iron*

this morning, date unknown,
seven books cover one side of the bed—
enough for a female constellation

black towel on hardwood floor
then crumpled trousers
then the mirror left leaning
accidentally at a perfect angle
to watch you light a cigarette
and fumble with your shoes

this evening you left
still wearing our shared sweat
I did not move my books
you did not ask

*Body/Orgy*

Washing buries but does not efface.
Flesh remains a palimpsest—
fingerprints, lips and curves pressed in.
Soap only smoothes brushstrokes.
They are in the skin.  They are of the body.
The lines are liquids
blended with liquids.
Lovers hold no hope that soap
will take away the nights
and let them bring only one body
to bed.  When a lover speaks,
a chorus speaks sweat, teeth,
muscle and breath.  We are never
alone in our embraces,
never alone outside them.
We are always clean in the night
as hungry roots drinking earth are clean.

*what we know of birth*

a bed brings out the new old

bodies fold and are folded

the skin lies by looking the same

the lightest touch folds
        exterior and interior, sends
        inside and outside
        beyond each other
        while it lingers

a hand on the stomach
        on the spine, thigh, cheek, ankle, shoulder
        blends another touch
        into what the skin conceals

a season of caresses
        folds a body into
        a freshly minted version of itself,
        a coin melted to make a coin

a body leaves the bed
        and contains one more face
        among yesterday's people

*All Woman*

How to tell her
I see
in every she
a wet fulcrum
bequeathed by
god's own engineer.
She is the whole
sorority
amalgamated,
yet light
as rising steam.
Omnipresence
flows from her
and I see,
under her touch,
the liquid signature
in every she.
She brings them in
under her skin.
I savor brief infidelity
in her embrace.
Which column
takes the mark
in the Promise Ledger?

*bark brings a body*

sipping your bark
brings a body
through the rings
to the sap

wary roots let you
amortize
advertise
collateralize
like some dead metal
that never was
a sapling
shocked by its first shiver
or bereft and grieving
falling leaves
before the truth of seasons
made loss banal

mouthful of splinters
and for you
what,
a mouthful of glass?

the bed is too soft
the floor is too hard

*Rush*

Crying. Raging. Half-mad.
To see, to catalog
every face fluttering
just beneath your skin
and waiting
for its own breeze
keeps me groping
for you in words
draped between
continents. A hand
feeds a breast when
a shoulder was sought,
or a thigh for a nape.
I can't tell whether
you're getting off
or getting angry, but
we still write
epistolary flesh for
half-empty beds
and place bets against
distance, time and speed.

# six

*a little extra*

A taxi idling in the driveway
sent out a short, polite honk—
a question, a warning.
She watched him dressing
from a bed still shedding his warmth.
He did not rush.
They had known the expiration date
from the beginning and had given
themselves fully to a fleeting union.
They had not missed or wasted
a moment or an opportunity.
As his taxi drove away
without him, he called a second—
honoring vows each would
one day make to another.
Those extra 15 minutes,
their golden years, were spent
silently memorizing a face before a face
for slow nights in the world
after their world.

*Aviary*

Before bed,
she read her diary aloud,
the morning's confessions
and captured dreams
becoming prayers.
Each cheap notebook
barely covered her palms.
She'd usher words
from these paper nests
and, without asking,
assume my silence.
This was her
wholeness ritual
before I shared her bed.
One word in ten
tumbled into me
and I kept each foundling,
shell intact,
for her to plunder
in the night.

*hide & seek*

forgive me
for loving you enough
to hate you
just a little
and for biting you
when I come
and for leaving
this confession
tucked into
your checkbook

*arcane technology*

She made me, let me . . . do things
I didn't know I desired.
Watelcané promised me your heart
if she could keep my body.
I caress you until I find
Watelcané's rhythm.  You are
the drum the tribe in my flesh
uses to call Watelcané to war
and peace.  What floods your thighs
is an offering at Watelcané's altar.
I love you before and after
but not during.  There, Watelcané steals
your breath and heat and folds her skin
between us.  She protects you
from the heavy bones and sharp teeth
she summons from my marrow.
Watelcané's jealousy
will put her claws
in our hearts if I speak her name.
I'm letting your morning coffee
brew exactly 6 minutes
in the French press I hate.
I will step outside for the paper
and burn this confession.
Watelcané will let you ask
if I've started smoking again
and smile when I say no.

*and I must let you sleep*

I pretend not to notice
the gun to my head. Its round mouth:
a lover's lips at my temple, a dove
resting under a canopy of hawks.
That barrel: winter's last
icy lash failing against green buds.
And I don't want the bullets
to be words, but they are
and they speak themselves
with the same cramped moan
I lost in an orchard with
my first orgasm, a sound
hushed by bees' wings and too feeble
to move the dust from my lips.
Your being asleep beside me
keeps each chamber loaded.
Your uncovered breast reveals
a hitch in your breath
that trembles the hammer.
Three inches between us—
a ravine, a ditch
where I need brickwork
to strain against instead of
commingled heat flattening
my fingertips when I forget.

*37 gray hairs*

Face and ass—both are visible
and exposed at this angle.
Broken capillary levees
on both cheeks
keep my eyes on your ass,
on the revealed flow of you;
I swim in that thick flood.
A voice evaporates
the pulsing current,
"What did you want to be
when you were a boy?"

We are sipping ice water
from glasses sweating against summer.
I keep watching
where your capillaries must
be healing themselves,
where broken architecture
is rebuilding arches and vaults.
Ice chimes against each glass,
marking hours in capillary time.
You stir and I still your calf
with a hand that no longer stings.
"I have to pee," you apologize.

I wanted to build robots.

*the minutes and hours*
*since we last made love*

this body, an
origami crane you
unfolded and left
flat, without volume
stripped down to
a thin landscape
strewn with overlapping
open folds, a
felled forest of lines
waiting for initiated fingers
to reconstruct root systems
exiled from thirst

*to give*

I left my keys,
the ones she'd given
as an unexplained present,
hanging from the scrap
of red silk and lace
she's skewered
with the key ring
to remind me of something.
I left my shirt
next to her gray cat
shielding its yellow eyes
from the day's
last blade of sunlight.
I left my shoes
with the socks inside
in the hall's elbow—
two black Italian leather moles
casting shadows on pale parquet.
I left my trousers
next to the portraits
mapping our history's
truces, cease-fires, armistices,
and occasional alliances.
I left my skin
hanging from the doorknob
so she might suspect
an invitation
down the line
where my small spaces
say *choose an atom*
*to crack open and spill out*
*flaming yolk.*

*lover*

Dog-eared your body's pages
and nearly cracked your spine.
Creased and folded you
where I needed
to remember my place
though you rewrite yourself
each time you flutter open
in my hands.  Your cover's
familiar signs of use and love
silence words galloping
in new lines and a new language.
Something in the pulp of you
preserves a few critical words
from your last edition.
These sweet saboteurs
push hands through eyes
and rewire your entire oeuvre.
Your reader races forward,
chasing behind your pen
and backward through past editions
made new.  You will slam shut
before your story finishes.
You will reshelve yourself,
leaving me your missing chapters
to invent and read
when I'm a bibliophile
alone in bed.

*Native Tongue*

To unfold
your crumpled voice
and put fire to its
pencil over ink over
failed erasures and edits
might help me listen
(in daylight and your absence)
to your genius,
the core that bucks you
against my face
and makes you risk
sliding back down the mountain
should my teeth nip
or neck cramp.
Your voice is acid
on my thinnest skin
etching away the alphabet
you rubbed into my marrow,
stealing my first words
in your native tongue.

*her only mole*

Lying in heat shed
by her sleeping engine,
he outlined her only mole,
watching how night's retreat
revealed expressions
in its crumpled face
linked directly
to nascent memories of her skin
suffused with luminosity
in varying degrees.

She pretended to sleep
as his sentinel finger
marched around and not over
her only mole.  She knew
he would persist,
staggering along sleep's border,
until she woke or turned.
She knew the mole's place
in his unseen architecture.
After absence or abstinence
assailed their tactile memories,
she'd catch him seeking
her only mole
to verify her
identity
as though she were
a fungible woman
simultaneously rare.

*Fever Music*

Vessel tipped back,
mouth sealing mouth,
you court fingers
on your softening label.
You grow light.
My throat admits nothing.
Thirst abates.

You sop my brow.
I'm speaking, and you mop away words.
Mop and wring.  I'm confessing.
You mop and scrub.  Skin on my forehead
molts where you work,
revealing iron and lead veins
cradling colored glass.
You help me mark
pathways out of flesh.
You reveal windows in my bones.

The factory knot in my belly
barely undone and you fly in
wrist deep.  Your fingers dance
in my carmine clockwork
like clown fish
snuggled in anemone.
I look away, shy
in my anticipation.
A bow and not a knot.
You promise you'll tie
a bow and not a knot.